*A LifeBuilder*

G000122756

# MOTHERHOOD
## *Being Grounded in Christ*

*10 studies*
*for individuals or groups*

Patty Pell

With Notes for Leaders

Scripture Union is an international Christian charity working with churches in more than 130 countries.

Thank you for purchasing this book. Any profits from this book support SU in England and Wales to bring the good news of Jesus Christ to children, young people and families and to enable them to meet God through the Bible and prayer.

Find out more about our work and how you can get involved at:

www.scriptureunion.org.uk (England and Wales)
www.suscotland.org.uk (Scotland)
www.suni.co.uk (Northern Ireland)
www.scriptureunion.org (USA)
www.su.org.au (Australia)

ISBN 978 1 84427 831 2

First published in the United States by InterVarsity Press.
First published in Great Britain by Scripture Union in 2013.

© Patty Pell

Printed in India by Thomson Press India Ltd.

# Contents

# Getting the Most Out of *Motherhood*

On the bookshelves of many mothers, you can find a myriad of titles related to parenting. There are books about nutrition during pregnancy, praying for unborn children, parenting infants and toddlers, disciplining strong personalities, engaging boys and empowering young girls, not to mention the titles about raising teenagers and adjusting to the empty nest. Some of these books are filled with highlighted paragraphs, notes and dog-eared pages. But many more of them are hardly touched and simply sit collecting dust. The amount of information, advice, to-do lists and instruction claiming to be the biblical way to parent and raise children is overwhelming and often discouraging and guilt inducing. I remember reaching for some parenting books early on in my days as a parent. There were a few that I could not have survived without, but there were many others that produced confusion, shame and guilt because I had chosen to discipline another way or to structure my child's schedule differently. The to-do lists were unrealistic and all-consuming.

I am not convinced that mothers need another book with advice on how to parent. There is a plethora of resources out there for those of us who desire more advice and instruction. But I *am* convinced that we mothers need to continually look at our internal worlds—the state of our souls, the health of our relationship with the Lord, and the growing or withering character of our personality. How we parent comes from who we are. The way we treat our children and the ways we respond in the joyful and the challenging aspects of being mothers are a reflection of our faith and our discipleship in the Lord Jesus.

For that reason, this study guide will not give you specifics on what to do with a difficult child or a moody teenager. It was not created to answer the questions of temper tantrums, puberty, peer pressure, academic success or substance abuse, and it will not give you a checklist for your day. This is intentional. Some women are called to be mothers, but as mothers we are also called to be disciples of Christ, neighbors, spouses, sisters, and some of us are additionally called to be teachers, businesswomen and doctors. Each of us has a unique situation and a unique calling. It is therefore impossible to address every circumstance and incident—and that's not what is needed.

What is needed is for us to allow the Holy Spirit to gently ask questions of identity, self-worth, unfulfilled hopes or expectations, unrealistic dreams, and issues of control and authority. This guide will facilitate that, creating space for Scripture to speak into our hearts and highlight some of our deepest needs: a growing and intimate relationship with Jesus, a heart of gratitude, a trust and faith in the goodness of the Lord, and a community of life-giving friends. The Lord desires us to grow as his children, placing our trust and faith in him, and as we do this in increasing ways through the crucible of parenting, we become more redeemed people. My desire for the study is that it would help us let God use the context of motherhood to form and shape us into the women he has created us to be, deepening who we are as people, as followers of Jesus and as parents.

## Suggestions for Individual Study

**1.** As you begin each study, pray that God will speak to you through his Word.

**2.** Read the introduction to the study and respond to the personal reflection question or exercise. This is designed to help you focus on God and on the theme of the study.

**3.** Each study deals with a particular passage so that you can delve into the author's meaning in that context. Read and reread the passage to be studied. The questions are written using the language of the New International Version, so you may wish to use that version of the Bible. The New Revised Standard Version is also recommended.

**4.** This is an inductive Bible study, designed to help you discover for yourself what Scripture is saying. The study includes three types of questions. Observation questions ask about the basic facts: who, what, when, where and how. Interpretation questions delve into the meaning of the passage. Application questions help you discover the implications of the text for growing in Christ. These three keys unlock the treasures of Scripture.

Write your answers to the questions in the spaces provided or in a personal journal. Writing can bring clarity and deeper understanding of yourself and of God's Word.

**5.** It might be good to have a Bible dictionary handy. Use it to look up any unfamiliar words, names or places.

**6.** Use the prayer suggestion to guide you in thanking God for what you have learned and to pray about the applications that have come to mind.

**7.** You may want to go on to the suggestion under "Now or Later," or you may want to use that idea for your next study.

## Suggestions for Members of a Group Study

**1.** Come to the study prepared. Follow the suggestions for individual study mentioned above. You will find that careful preparation will greatly enrich your time spent in group discussion.

**2.** Be willing to participate in the discussion. The leader of your group will not be lecturing. Instead, he or she will be encouraging the members of the group to discuss what they have learned. The leader will be asking the questions that are found in this guide.

**3.** Stick to the topic being discussed. Your answers should be based on the verses which are the focus of the discussion and not on outside authorities such as commentaries or speakers. These studies focus on a particular passage of Scripture. Only rarely should you refer to other portions of the Bible. This allows for everyone to participate in in-depth study on equal ground.

**4.** Be sensitive to the other members of the group. Listen attentively when they describe what they have learned. You may be surprised by their insights! Each question assumes a variety of answers. Many questions do not have "right" answers, particularly questions that aim at meaning or application. Instead the questions push us to explore the passage more thoroughly.

When possible, link what you say to the comments of others. Also, be affirming whenever you can. This will encourage some of the more hesitant members of the group to participate.

**5.** Be careful not to dominate the discussion. We are sometimes so eager to express our thoughts that we leave too little opportunity for others to respond. By all means participate! But allow others to also.

**6.** Expect God to teach you through the passage being discussed and through the other members of the group. Pray that you will have an enjoyable and profitable time together, but also that as a result of the study you will find ways that you can take action individually and/or as a group.

**7.** Remember that anything said in the group is considered confidential and should not be discussed outside the group unless specific permission is given to do so.

**8.** If you are the group leader, you will find additional suggestions at the back of the guide.

# 1

# The Secure Mother

*Finding Our Identity in Christ*

## Ephesians 1:3-14

Really only one thing helps me maintain my integrity and composure at soccer games or volleyball matches: sitting as close as possible to the opposing team's fans. It serves as a much needed barrier against my rants and ravings! If I have to sit next to the parent of another child, they become real and personal. It's much more difficult after that to demonize the other team, scream at the ref or complain about my child's playing time.

My responses at athletic competitions represent an area in need of constant redemption. I begin every game by telling myself I'll be positive, encouraging and quiet. Yet at every game I struggle to do just that. I can justify my agitation by saying I just want my child to do well and to succeed, but it goes much deeper than that. What's at the root of my behavior? If my son succeeds, then I succeed. And if I succeed I am worth something. I am valuable. Our identity is so often misplaced. Who can rescue us?

GROUP DISCUSSION. In what ways do you feel insecure as a mother? What makes you anxious or worried?

PERSONAL REFLECTION. Trying to be as honest with yourself as possible, how do you think God sees you or feels about you?

The first chapter of the book of Ephesians is a theological gem, in part because it answers the question of who we are. The true answer to that question is one we can't hear enough. *Read Ephesians 1:3-14.*

---

**1.** When you hear the phrase "spiritual blessings," what are some thoughts that come to mind?

---

**2.** List the blessings that Paul names in this passage that God has given his people.

---

**3.** What do verses 3-10 reveal about God's heart and emotions toward his people?

---

**4.** How does the image of adoption help us understand our relationship with God?

**5.** In what ways do we as mothers try to earn God's love and impress others in order to feel secure?

_____

**6.** How do verses 3-10 help us set aside our insecurity and self-doubt in our parenting?

_____

**7.** Identify some mistakes and regrets you have from this past week as a mum. How does the truth that we have redemption and the forgiveness of sins (v. 7) affect those memories?

_____

**8.** How does Paul describe the purpose of God's activity in the world in verses 9-14?

_____

**9.** How can this eternal and all-encompassing view of God's purpose in the world transform our daily lives as mothers?

**10.** In verses 11-14 Paul reminds us that the Holy Spirit is our deposit and the guarantee that we will inherit redemption. How do you see the presence of the Holy Spirit in your life as a mum?

**11.** Think back to the personal reflection or group discussion question at the beginning of the study. What aspect of this passage in Ephesians speaks most powerfully to the area in your life you described in that question?

**12.** This passage is filled with the lavishness of God toward us. Think about either a specific way you need to experience his lavishness or a way you can lavish his love on your children this week.

*Pray in an attitude of thankfulness for all the blessings that have been described in this passage. Thank the Lord for the specific ways in which these blessings have been seen in your life.*

### Now or Later

Read Colossians 1:15-20. Reflect on the power and authority of the Lord Jesus Christ. How does this picture of Jesus help you cope with the challenges of motherhood?

# 2

# The Healing Mother

*Acknowledging Our Own Issues*

## Mark 5:21-43

"I want my daughter to have all the newest equipment because I didn't have it when I was growing up." These words spoken by a friend of mine provided a window into her wounded soul.

Everyone experiences emotional, physical or spiritual pain throughout their life. It might come from bullying we've faced, abandonment, racist comments or jokes, or physical limitations. Whatever the wound, the effects stay with us and can then affect the way we parent. My friend, for example, had felt embarrassment as a teen in the midst of other teens with more means and now years later she was making financial decisions for her family out of a place of brokenness and pain.

The truth is that denying or ignoring the places of pain in our past and present only leads to more pain and brokenness. As a mother, then, one of the most important things we can do is be honest and open about the places of hurt in our lives and open ourselves up to the healing power of the Holy Spirit.

GROUP DISCUSSION. What is one thing you would like to change about how you parent?

PERSONAL REFLECTION. If you could change something about your childhood, what would it be? How has that experience affected the way you parent?

Mark 5 is a moving story of people in pain and desperation journeying to Christ. And it is a picture of how mothers might move forward in their own healing to break the cycle of pain for their children. *Read Mark 5:21-34.*

---

**1.** Picture yourself in this scene. What do you see, hear and experience as a person in this story?

---

**2.** What do we know about Jairus and the bleeding woman from this passage?

---

**3.** In what ways are Jairus and the woman similar and different?

---

**4.** What risks do the woman and Jairus take in their desperation?

**5.** Jairus and the woman come to Jesus for healing from their respective wounds. What wounds do you feel are still very raw and open in your own life?

---

**6.** How do these areas of pain affect you as a mother?

---

**7.** What would it look like for you to come to Jesus with these wounds?

---

**8.** Picture what motherhood might be like if these wounds did not hold so much power in your life. What do you envision?

---

**9.** Reread verses 35-43. How are Jesus' interactions with Jairus and the woman similar, and how are they different?

**10.** How does Jesus heal the physical, emotional and spiritual wounds in this story?

---

**11.** Looking inside to our emotional and spiritual wounds and deficits is difficult and unsettling (vv. 33, 36). What fears do you have in exposing your pain and wounds to Jesus and asking for healing?

---

**12.** What step might you need to take this week to identify your wounds and bring them to Jesus?

*Pray about the wounds that came up in this study. If you're doing this in a group, divide into pairs and spend some time praying for each other.*

### Now or Later

Many times our wounds have been passed on in our families through generations. Spend some time this week reflecting on the patterns of sin and pain that you see in your family. Then pray that the Lord will break the cycle for you and your children.

# 3

# The Trusting Mother

*Depending on God*

## Matthew 6:25-34

In the nineties certain 3-D posters made up of geometric shapes and patterns were all the rage. If you stared at one in the right way for the right amount of time, suddenly a picture appeared (usually gardens or cityscapes or animals), but there was no hint of the picture when you first looked at the geometric patterns. It was the act of focusing through and beyond the pattern that enabled the brain to see the picture in it.

Those pictures are a fabulous metaphor for the spiritual life. We can be so distracted by the present reality—the patterns and geometric shapes of our current circumstances—that we are blind to the wondrous gifts lying just beyond. Only when we're able to focus on the right thing can we move beyond the anxieties and worry of the present and see the beauty and truth before us. But what is it that we have to focus on? What will help us overcome the constant barrage of things to worry about? Jesus gives us the answer in a section of his Sermon on the Mount.

GROUP DISCUSSION. Describe the cycle of worry in your life: what triggers worry or anxiety, how are you affected by it and how is the worry resolved?

PERSONAL REFLECTION. Think about the last week. What were the things that caused you stress or worry?

After Jesus calls his disciples to follow him, he describes in his Sermon on the Mount what it means to be a follower of Christ and how life in the kingdom of God is different. His words are relevant for all people and certainly something we as mothers need to hear! *Read Matthew 6:25-34.*

**1.** What are all the areas and details in the passage that Jesus challenges his audience not to worry about?

**2.** How are birds and flowers similar to and different from people?

**3.** In Jesus' instructions to not worry about our life (v. 25), he specifically mentions the daily worries most relevant to his audience: eating and drinking. What life details do you worry about most in your present circumstances?

**4.** How does Jesus show the futility of worrying about our lives in verse 27?

**5.** In his instructions not to worry about our bodies, Jesus specifically mentions what a person wears. How do you experience anxiety related to your body?

**6.** Read Matthew 6:24. In what ways are this verse and verses 25-34 connected?

**7.** How does Jesus contrast pagans and the people of God in verses 32-34?

**8.** Describe what someone who is seeking first the kingdom of God would be like. What character traits come to mind? What lifestyle do you envision them having? How do you think they would make decisions?

---

**9.** How does seeking the kingdom and the righteousness of God first help us avoid worrying about tomorrow?

---

**10.** Mothers have many worries related to their own lives, bodies and futures, but they also have unique anxieties connected to being a mum. What are some worries that you think are unique to motherhood?

---

**11.** Think back to the opening questions and your own cycle of worry. What would it mean to seek first the kingdom of God and his righteousness in those specific areas of anxiety?

**12.** Choose one specific way in which you could set aside a worry about money, your life, your body or your future or worries about your family this week by seeking God first.

*Set aside a few moments of silence to ask God what worries are interfering with your ability to seek and follow him. Listen for his compassionate voice. Then spend some time in prayer for yourself and for other mums you know.*

## Now or Later

Here are some ways you might intentionally seek God's help in the area of worry this week:

**1.** Journal about some of the recurring worries in your life and try to identify, through the power of the Holy Spirit, what the root fears or causes might be.

**2.** Talk with some of the members of your family of origin about their constant worries. Journal and pray about how you have inherited some of the same patterns.

**3.** Through prayer and discussion with family, try to identify some of the triggers for certain worries. How can you be aware of those triggers and choose to seek God in those moments?

# 4

# The Wonder-Filled Mother

*Gaining Perspective*

## Psalm 139:1-18

Many mothers experience a special moment, after the pain and anxiety of labor and delivery are over, of holding their newborn and feeling at peace. Adoptive mothers experience a similar moment when the waiting is over and they are finally holding their new child. In those moments, it doesn't matter what is happening around the mother. She is singularly focused on this new life, and full of wonder and amazement—wonder at the whole process of child-bearing, at the miracle of life and at this small person, in particular. And yet the baby hasn't even done anything! The child's simple presence is a cause for wonder and amazement.

How quickly that sense of wonder fades as children grow. Soon parents are pushing their kids to perform and accomplish. Too soon, parents are frustrated and worried about their children's personalities, behavior, lack of accolades or interests. What happens? Where does the wonder go? And how does the absence of this wonder affect us as mothers and as people?

GROUP DISCUSSION. Think of someone who knows you extremely well. Describe this relationship.

PERSONAL REFLECTION. Reflect on the characteristics of yourself that you enjoy. With what people or in what circumstances do those characteristics shine the most?

Often attributed to King David, Psalm 139 is both an intensely personal description of the nearness of God and a lofty treatment of his all-present, all-powerful nature. It can become a foundational Scripture passage for mothers, teaching us to stop and reflect on the wonders of life and motherhood. *Read Psalm 139:1-18.*

1. What are the topics that the psalmist moves in and out of in these verses?

2. Verse 6 is the psalmist's response to the truth about God's knowledge described in verses 1-5. What words and phrases would you use to respond to verses 1-5?

**3.** What do verses 7-12 reveal about God's character?

**4.** How are you affected by the psalmist's statements about God's presence in verses 7-12?

**5.** What do these verses about God's knowledge and constant presence mean to you as a mother?

**6.** Insert the names of your children in these verses in place of the personal pronouns (*me, I, my,* etc.). How does this change your perspective of your children, of parenting or even of yourself?

**7.** What do verses 13-18 teach about God's creation?

**8.** Describe one aspect of how God created you that is a strength in motherhood.

**9.** God has fearfully and wonderfully made our children as well. What qualities of your children do you delight in?

**10.** What does verse 16 say about the present and the future?

**11.** This psalm is designed to create in us a sense of wonder. What about being a mother stirs in you a sense of wonder?

**12.** Choose one verse from this psalm that stands out to you. What might God be saying to you through this verse? You may want to commit to meditating on the verse in the coming week.

*Praise God for the many ways he has wonderfully created you and your children. Allow the Spirit to bring to mind qualities about your children or yourself that he loves and delights in but perhaps you overlook or discount.*

**Now or Later**

A few suggestions for growing in wonder during the coming week:

**1.** Make a list of all the things about each of your children that fills you with wonder. Regularly pray through that list, giving thanks to God. Write little notes to your children affirming these qualities in them.

**2.** Rewrite verses 7-12 with the "if's" that make you fearful. After each "if," write a statement about God's presence and faithfulness.

**3.** Write a list of the qualities in yourself that you enjoy. Pray through that list, asking God to help you embrace these things.

**4.** Make a commitment to avoid saying negative things about yourself. Ask God to help you stop "cursing" yourself with critical words.

# 5

# The Growing Mother

*Nurturing Ourselves,*

## Romans 12:1-8

"I didn't have any idea I liked high school students until I had my own," my friend told me on the phone the other day as she described her passion for a new ministry. Lynn has sought out God's leading in her life and invested herself in the work of the kingdom in every stage of parenting. She was on the mission field, she worked in a business office part time, she stayed at home to raise her kids when they were little, and now with several off to college and one in high school, she has been trying her hand at tutoring refugee students in the public high school. In this new ministry and in the many others she's engaged in, Lynn has beautifully allowed God to use her gifts and to stir new passions and interests in her as her life has unfolded. Lynn epitomizes a growing mother!

GROUP DISCUSSION. How has being a mother affected your relationship with the Lord? How has your relationship with him changed positively and/or negatively?

PERSONAL REFLECTION. Reflect on the current condition of your relationship with the Lord. How would you describe it?

The apostle Paul spends the first eleven chapters of Romans making his theological case for our salvation by the grace of God through faith in Jesus Christ. In chapter 12, Paul begins to apply this theological understanding to the church. Verses 1-8 are a challenge to believers to embrace their God-given gifts and talents, and to employ them in the body of Christ and in the world. This same challenge applies to women in their days of motherhood. *Read Romans 12:1-8.*

---

**1.** Identify the words, phrases or ideas that Paul repeats in these verses. What contrasts does he make?

---

**2.** What might Paul mean when he urges the believers to offer their bodies as a living sacrifice in verse 1?

---

**3.** Since becoming a mother, what in your life may have held you back from the Lord?

---

**4.** Paul contrasts living by the pattern of the world with living as transformed people (v. 2). Describe what this kind of transformation looks like.

**5.** The transformation Paul's referring to comes about by the renewing of our mind. How do we renew our minds?

---

**6.** What are some of the consequences of neglecting the things that help us renew our minds and be transformed?

---

**7.** What is one specific step that you can take to facilitate the renewal of your mind?

---

**8.** Paul repeats the phrase "do not" twice (vv. 2-3). How are they connected?

---

**9.** In what ways are we as mothers unrealistic about ourselves? What could it look like for us to see ourselves with "sober judgment" instead?

**10.** What does Paul mean when he says that "each member be-longs to all the others"?

**11.** How has the use of your spiritual gifts changed since be-coming a mother?

**12.** As you have been going through this study, what might God be saying to you about your gifts or your stage of motherhood?

*Ask God to meet you as you practice the discipline you chose in question seven. If you're doing this study in a group, divide into pairs or triads and pray for each other. Then talk about how you can follow up in prayer for one another in the coming week.*

### Now or Later

Ideas for nurturing your own growth:

**1.** Take a spiritual gifts inventory as a way of discovering your spiritual gifts, reminding yourself of them or seeing if they have changed a bit over time.

**2.** Find an older mum who has continued to have a signifi-cant impact on the kingdom as she has gone through life and motherhood. Ask her if she will mentor you.

# 6

# The Free Mother

## Letting Go of Expectations

Psalm 131

I found myself wandering through hundreds of high school seniors and their parents at a downtown Chicago hotel. Around me, vocalists were warming up their voices, dancers were stretching and aspiring actors were quietly rehearsing monologues. I was with my daughter at national auditions for performing arts college programs. As the two days unfolded, I could feel the level of tension and anxiety in myself and in other parents increase exponentially. Some of the conversations around me were filled with palpable worry as parents whispered instructions to their child while also talking about the specific aspirations they had for their son or daughter. I began to wonder if my husband and I had researched enough, planned thoroughly enough, strategized effectively or followed the right path.

In other conversations, parents were laughing, reminding their son or daughter everything would be just fine. Peace and pleasure replaced the intensity. I breathed a sigh of relief when I found myself outside audition rooms with these parents. But how was it that some parents seemed at ease with the outcome for their child while others were wracked with stress? Psalm 131 helps us understand.

GROUP DISCUSSION. How would you define *ambition*? Is ambition something Christians should cultivate?

PERSONAL REFLECTION. In what areas of your life are you tempted to "rule the roost," meddle or control things?

Psalm 131 is one of the "Songs of Ascent" (Psalms 120–132), songs the Israelites used regularly as they journeyed to and from Jerusalem for feasts and festivals. These psalms were a tool of discipleship that taught the people how to be the people of God. Psalm 131 can serve as a similar tool for us. *Read Psalm 131.*

1. Charles Spurgeon said of this psalm, "It is one of the shortest Psalms to read, but one of the longest to learn." What contrasts do you find in these few verses?

2. What images come to mind when you read verse 1?

3. Describe the difference between the "ambition" that the psalmist suggests is negative and "aspiration," which might be positive. How are you tempted by ambition (in general and as a mother)?

4. Describe the characteristics of a weaned child.

5. The psalmist seems to be distinguishing an unhealthy demanding from childlike trust. What do each of those postures look like?

6. Think of your role as a mother. How do you approach God as a child who has not been weaned?

7. Rate your "contentment" with God on a scale of one to ten, with one being "not content at all" and ten being "perfectly content." What contributes to the ranking you gave?

8. In what area(s) do you long to feel "stilled and quieted"?

**9.** Identify one expectation or desire that you have been hold-ing onto related to your role as a mother or related to one of your children. What would it mean for you to let that go and trust in the Lord?

*Sit in silence and stillness for several minutes asking God to calm and quiet you. Bask in God's presence without any requests or demands.*

## Now or Later

A few suggestions for you for this day or in the coming week:

**1.** Identifying our expectations and hidden agendas for our children can be difficult and painful. Spend some time journal-ing about those expectations. If your children are old enough, you may want to ask them what unrealistic expectations or pressure they feel from you.

**2.** Practice the discipline of contentment by praying a prayer of thanksgiving at the end of each day. Try rejoicing only in who God has been in your life that day, not on the "deeds" he has done for you.

# 7

# The Humble Mother

*Walking in Grace*

## Luke 18:9-14

When my oldest daughter was an infant, some mothers were using terms like "the biblical way" or "God's way" to describe the choices that they were making about things like how often to feed their infant, whether to pick up a crying child from the crib and how to get an infant to sleep through the night. Other mothers were convinced of the goodness and necessity of bonding with their infant through a family bed, paying attention to the cries of an infant at all times, and constantly holding and nurturing the child. Both sides claimed to know the right way to parent, and accusations and critique flew back and forth. (These debates still occur today, but the intensity of these conversations ebbs and flows.) The end result, unfortunately, was a lot of mothers who were left feeling guilty, judged and regretful about decisions they had made. What was missing in many of the debates was a sense of grace and humility.

GROUP DISCUSSION. Describe the last time you "bragged" about your children. Who were you talking with, what did you say, and how were you feeling?

PERSONAL REFLECTION. What about your children fills you with pride?

Judgment and arrogance have no place in the kingdom of God, yet we practice them frequently. They seep out of a well of self-righteousness. And Jesus had a lot to say about self-righteousness. *Read Luke 18:9-14.*

**1.** What two characteristics of Jesus' audience does Luke highlight (v. 1)?

How are those two characteristics connected?

**2.** Who were the Pharisees and the tax collectors?

**3.** How does the Pharisee in Jesus' parable view himself?

**4.** Name all the contrasts you can find between the tax collector and the Pharisee.

**5.** As a mother, which character in the story do you identify with the most? Why?

---

**6.** We all have a tendency at some point to have confidence in our own righteousness and to judge others because of it. Rewrite the words of the Pharisee in verse 11 from your own perspective: "God, I thank you that I am not like . . ."

---

**7.** Why would the end of the parable (v. 14) have been a surprise to Jesus' audience?

---

**8.** What does it mean to exalt yourself? To humble yourself?

---

**9.** How have exalting and humbling yourself affected relationships with other women in your life?

**10.** How is this parable a story of freedom for us as mothers?

*The reminder of our need for God's mercy helps to ground us in the correct perspective. Spend several minutes in private confession using the words of the tax collector from the passage: "God, have mercy on me, a sinner."*

*Then sit in silence and ask the Lord to show you ways in which you rely on your own righteousness. As things come to mind, confess those to the Lord and ask for his mercy.*

### Now or Later

Here a few exercises that can help move us toward the humility God desires:

**1.** Study Philippians 2:5-11. What do humility and exaltation look like in this passage? In what ways can you apply this same exhortation to the other mothers in your life?

**2.** The next time you are aware of judging another mother or parent, take a moment to reflect on the motivation behind the judgment. Why are you comparing yourself? What does your response to this person and to this situation say about you? How is God speaking to you in this instance?

# 8

# The Connected Mother

*Finding Community*

**Colossians 3:1-17**

In his book *Go and Do*, Don Everts uses airline safety guidelines as an example of our need to abide in Christ. Flight attendants explain that, if the cabin air pressure drops and air masks become necessary, parents should place a mask on themselves first before placing one on their child. Our initial response to this is often indignation. *How can parents put their own safety ahead of their children's?* But, as Don points out, "it doesn't matter how much you love your child if you pass out while trying to put her mask on her." As mothers we urgently need to grasp the truth of this in relation to our own spiritual health. It doesn't matter how much we love our children if we ignore our own emotional and spiritual health. At some point, the air pressure will change and we will pass out—and we'll then be unable to place a life-saving air mask on our child. How do we learn to care for ourselves?

One crucial aspect of caring for ourselves is realizing we desperately need deep, trust-filled relationships. We need to experience a Christian community where we are loved, celebrated and known, and where we can love and celebrate others as well. Community can be that oxygen mask that supports us as mothers so that we can give ourselves to our calling as mothers.

GROUP DISCUSSION. Think about the friendships in your life right now. How would you rate them on a scale of one to five, with one being "not at all life-giving" and five being "very life-giving"? What made you choose this number?

PERSONAL REFLECTION. What is one characteristic of yourself that is an asset to relationships with friends? What is one characteristic of yourself that needs the Lord's redemption with regard to the relationships in your life?

In Colossians 3, Paul addresses the need for the church to live in community, to stay connected. For us as mothers, connection with others is a lifeline that can—sometimes literally—save us and our children. *Read Colossians 3:1-17.*

1. Identify all the cause-and-effect relationships in this passage. Key words to look for include *because, therefore* and *since.*

2. According to Paul, what were the Colossians like in the past, before Christ?

**3.** How would you paraphrase Paul's description of how the present reality of the Colossian believers is different from their past?

---

**4.** Paul uses three key verbs to structure this passage: *set, put* and *let.* How do these words emphasize different aspects of living as a believer in community?

---

**5.** Which of the three verbs (*set, put, let*) do you struggle with the most in your own life and in your role as a parent?

---

**6.** Why is verse 11 so important to Paul's argument in this text?

---

**7.** How does understanding that we're chosen and dearly loved help us as God's people to live according to verses 12-14?

**8.** Which of the character traits mentioned in verses 12-14 would you like to see increased in your life?

Why did you choose that particular trait?

---

**9.** What makes it hard for mothers to engage in community or to find a community like what's described in this passage?

---

**10.** How would having a community of believers like this around you affect your role as a mother?

---

**11.** Paul ends this section of the letter to the Colossians with words about thankfulness. Why are gratitude and expressions of thanksgiving crucial to our life, especially as women and mothers?

*Give thanks and gratitude to the Lord for whatever comes to mind. You can spend the whole prayer time in thanksgiving if you want to. If you feel the need to move on, though, spend a few minutes praying for other mums you're in relationship with.*

**Now or Later**

A few ideas for understanding and experiencing community:

**1.** Study some of the passages in Paul's other letters that are parallel texts to Colossians 3, such as Galatians 3:23-28 or Ephesians 4.

**2.** If you have been doing this study on your own and do not have a community, make some specific plans to find a place of community. This might mean joining a small group at church or some other ministry, or initiating a time with some friends to get together and pray for one another.

# 9

# The Influencing Mother

*Leaving a Legacy*

There was an entertaining but also informative board game back in the eighties called Careers. At the beginning of the game, each player had to decide on his or her individual life plan by choosing stars (fame), hearts (happiness) and dollar signs (wealth) until they had a total of sixty units. Each player then moved around the board entering the various paths of either occupation or education. Along the way, surprises like "You just landed on the moon; you receive ten stars" would occur. The profound part of the game was that each player had to decide which paths to take or retake based on the life formula he or she set out at the start of the game.

The game has always been a helpful reminder to me of how we approach life and of how we tend to approach parenting. If we're not sure how we want to influence our children or what kind of legacy we hope to leave in their lives, we'll approach parenting reactively, with less thought about how our reactions and decisions in the present will affect the future. When we know and are committed to our "life formula," we will interact with our children, make decisions about our time and energy, and even discipline our children intentionally in ways that pursue the kind of influence we long for.

GROUP DISCUSSION. Describe someone in your life who has impacted you spiritually. What was it about this person that affected you so meaningfully?

PERSONAL REFLECTION. Reflect on the impact of either your mother or father in your life. Where has there been positive impact? How has your mother or father invested in you? If your relationship with your mother or father is a painful one, reflect on how that brokenness has affected your desire to influence your children.

In 1 Thessalonians 1, Paul praises the church for how they have become models of the gospel. He spends chapter 2 outlining the ways he, Silas and Timothy were able to influence the Thessalonians and leave a legacy of faithfulness to Christ. His words are an inspiration and challenge for us as mothers today. *Read 1 Thessalonians 2:1-12.*

**1.** For a bit of context, read 1 Thessalonians 1:3, 7-8. How would you describe the spiritual lives and ministry of the Thessalonians?

**2.** Moving back to chapter 2, what does it mean that Paul, Silas and Timothy "dared to tell" the gospel to the Thessalonians (v. 2)?

---

**3.** In what ways do you struggle to "dare to tell" the gospel?

---

**4.** This passage vividly describes the ways in which Paul, Silas and Timothy invested in the lives of the Thessalonian believers. What do verses 3-6 tell us about the motives of these men?

---

**5.** Describe some of the impure or unhealthy motivations that tend to find their way into our relationships, ministry and parenting.

---

**6.** What familial images does Paul use in verses 7-12 to describe his method of discipling or investing in the Thessalonians?

**7.** Which familial image fits your personality the best?

Which image do you struggle with?

---

**8.** Where do you see the idea of modeling in this passage?

---

**9.** This text is a beautiful picture of how Paul, Silas and Timothy invested in a young church. They had pure motives. They loved, nurtured, exhorted and challenged the believers. They modeled the Christian life, refusing to abuse authority, power or position. And they did this without seeking the praise of people—only that of God. What is your response when you think of having this kind of relationship with your children?

---

**10.** What does this passage teach us about the nature of "legacy"?

**11.** What would it look like to intentionally invest in the spiritual life of your children?

What is one thing that you can focus on this week toward this goal?

*Pray for your children. You might want to spend a few minutes in silence asking God to speak to you about the specific qualities he wants to increase in the lives of your children.*

### Now or Later

Use these ideas to help you think intentionally about leaving a legacy for your children:

**1.** Study the lives of Moses and Joshua in the following passages: Exodus 17:8-14, Exodus 33:1-17, Numbers 14:5-9 and Joshua 1:1-19. How did Moses develop Joshua as a leader?

**2.** Spend some time reflecting and journaling about the impure motives in your life as a parent. Pray through these with a trusted friend.

# 10

# The Joyful Mother

*Living in Gratitude*

## Philippians 4:4-9

When I occasionally speak at conferences or meetings out of town, I love to talk about my family, especially my children, as a way of introducing myself to the group. The act of trying to describe each of my three children is an exercise in gratitude because they are so different and so enjoyable in their own way; I always feel that I'm giving glory to the creativity of God the Father as I seek to capture my children in a few sentences. My oldest daughter is compassionate, soft-hearted and deeply emotional, and she engages life through art and narrative. My son is athletic, sweet and charismatic, and wanders through life with a gorgeous and contagious smile. My youngest daughter is witty, sarcastic and comedic, and approaches life casually with ease. These characteristic were hard to see when they were young, but as they have grown and matured, the creative way in which God has woven each of their personalities together has emerged. I am so thankful for each of them.

It is not always easy to be grateful or to focus on the lovely, noble, creative aspects of our children, ourselves or the circumstances of our life. But being thankful works wonders in staving off the destructive nature of complaint and grumbling. And it's a life-giving exercise—one that springs from the joy the Holy Spirit deposits in us.

GROUP DISCUSSION. Think of someone in your life who seems to be a joyful person. How does that person's attitude affect you?

PERSONAL REFLECTION. Describe the last time that you truly rejoiced about something.

The book of Philippians reveals a deep relationship of partnership and love between Paul and the Philippian church. Throughout his letter Paul encourages the church to continue to grow in their faith no matter what the consequences. His words offer essential perspective for us as mothers. *Read Philippians 4:4-9.*

---

**1.** The words of these verses have been quoted often by believers over the centuries. What makes theses six verses so powerful?

---

**2.** Paul is ending his letter to the Philippians here, which means these thoughts are some of the ones he most wants his fellow believers to embrace. How do these verses paint a picture of a truly correct and healthy way of living?

**3.** Paul begins this section by once again reminding the church to rejoice. What does it mean to "rejoice in the Lord always"?

**4.** According to verses 4-6, how should we approach prayer?

**5.** In the middle of verses 4-7 Paul states that "the Lord is near." How does this truth affect our ability to rejoice and to pray with thanksgiving?

**6.** Think about your children for a moment. What can you rejoice in about them this very day?

**7.** Reflect on the content of the prayers that you normally present to God about your children. How might they change if you presented your requests with a joyful heart and with thanksgiving?

**8.** Describe what happens in our own lives when we do the opposite of what Paul encourages and focus on lies and what is ugly, broken and negative.

**9.** How does our focus on the negative affect our children, whether we are being negative about them, about ourselves or about life?

**10.** What is one way that you can focus on what's true, noble, right, pure, lovely or admirable in your life this week?

**11.** Parenting is (obviously!) an extremely challenging under-taking. What is one thing you've learned about yourself in the process that you're thankful to have learned?

**12.** Think back on what you have seen, learned or received from this study of motherhood. What is one thing that you desire to put into practice in your life as a mother with the help of the Holy Spirit?

*It is appropriate that this study ends with rejoicing and thanksgiving, so spend time praising God for the wonderful qualities of your children and the things that you have learned as a mother. Be diligent to remain in thanksgiving, focusing on what is true, noble and lovely.*

### Now or Later

A few suggestions for the week ahead:

**1.** Commit for a week to offer every petition and request to God only through thanksgiving.

**2.** If you are going through a painful or difficult time, ask God to reveal the things in the situation that you can rejoice about. Spend some time in listening prayer as God speaks to you.

**3.** Go back through the study, reflecting and praying about the things you learned and the ways God spoke to you through his Word.

# Leader's Notes

*MY GRACE IS SUFFICIENT FOR YOU. (2 COR 12:9)*

Leading a Bible discussion can be an enjoyable and rewarding experience. But it can also be *scary*—especially if you've never done it before. If this is your feeling, you're in good company. When God asked Moses to lead the Israelites out of Egypt, he replied, "O Lord, please send someone else to do it!" (Ex 4:13). It was the same with Solomon, Jeremiah and Timothy, but God helped these people in spite of their weaknesses, and he will help you as well.

You don't need to be an expert on the Bible or a trained teacher to lead a Bible discussion. The idea behind these inductive studies is that the leader guides group members to discover for themselves what the Bible has to say. This method of learning will allow group members to remember much more of what is said than a lecture would.

These studies are designed to be led easily. As a matter of fact, the flow of questions through the passage from observation to interpretation to application is so natural that you may feel that the studies lead themselves. This study guide is also flexible. You can use it with a variety of groups—student, professional, neighborhood or church groups. Each study takes forty-five to sixty minutes in a group setting.

There are some important facts to know about group dynamics and encouraging discussion. The suggestions listed below should enable you to effectively and enjoyably fulfill your role as leader.

### Preparing for the Study

**1.** Ask God to help you understand and apply the passage in your own life. Unless this happens, you will not be prepared to lead others. Pray too for the various members of the group. Ask God to open your hearts to the message of his Word and motivate you to action.

**2.** Read the introduction to the entire guide to get an overview of the entire book and the issues which will be explored.

**3.** As you begin each study, read and reread the assigned Bible passage to familiarize yourself with it.

**4.** This study guide is based on the New International Version of the Bible. It will help you and the group if you use this translation as the basis for your study and discussion.

**5.** Carefully work through each question in the study. Spend time in meditation and reflection as you consider how to respond.

**6.** Write your thoughts and responses in the space provided in the study guide. This will help you to express your understanding of the passage clearly.

**7.** It might help to have a Bible dictionary handy. Use it to look up any unfamiliar words, names or places. (For additional help on how to study a passage, see chapter five of *How to Lead a LifeGuide Bible Study,* InterVarsity Press.)

**8.** Consider how you can apply the Scripture to your life. Remember that the group will follow your lead in responding to the studies. They will not go any deeper than you do.

**9.** Once you have finished your own study of the passage, familiarize yourself with the leader's notes for the study you are leading. These are designed to help you in several ways. First, they tell you the purpose the study guide author had in mind when writing the study. Take time to think through how the study questions work together to accomplish that purpose. Second, the notes provide you with additional background information or suggestions on group dynamics for various questions. This information can be useful when people have difficulty understanding or answering a question. Third, the leader's notes can alert you to potential problems you may encounter during the study.

**10.** If you wish to remind yourself of anything mentioned in the leader's notes, make a note to yourself below that question in the study.

## Leading the Study

**1.** Begin the study on time. Open with prayer, asking God to help the group to understand and apply the passage.

**2.** Be sure that everyone in your group has a study guide. Encourage the group to prepare beforehand for each discussion by reading the introduction to the guide and by working through the questions in the study.

**3.** At the beginning of your first time together, explain that these studies are meant to be discussions, not lectures. Encourage the members of the group to participate. However, do not put pressure on those who may be hesitant to speak during the first few sessions. You may want to suggest the following guidelines to your group.

☐ Stick to the topic being discussed.

☐ Your responses should be based on the verses which are the focus of the discussion and not on outside authorities such as commentaries or speakers.

☐ These studies focus on a particular passage of Scripture. Only rarely should you refer to other portions of the Bible. This allows for everyone to participate in in-depth study on equal ground.

☐ Anything said in the group is considered confidential and will not be discussed outside the group unless specific permission is given to do so.

☐ We will listen attentively to each other and provide time for each person present to talk.

☐ We will pray for each other.

**4.** Have a group member read the introduction at the beginning of the discussion.

**5.** Every session begins with a group discussion question. The question or activity is meant to be used before the passage is read. The question introduces the theme of the study and encourages group members to begin to open up. Encourage as many members as possible to participate, and be ready to get the discussion going with your own response.

This section is designed to reveal where our thoughts or feelings need to be transformed by Scripture. That is why it is especially important not to read the passage before the discussion question is asked. The passage will tend to color the honest reactions people would otherwise give because they are, of course, supposed to think the way the Bible does.

You may want to supplement the group discussion question with an icebreaker to help people to get comfortable. See the community section of *Small Group Idea Book* for more ideas.

You also might want to use the personal reflection question with your group. Either allow a time of silence for people to respond individually or discuss it together.

**6.** Have a group member (or members if the passage is long) read aloud the passage to be studied. Then give people several minutes to read the passage again silently so that they can take it all in.

**7.** Question 1 will generally be an overview question designed to briefly survey the passage. Encourage the group to look at the whole passage, but try to avoid getting sidetracked by questions or issues that will be addressed later in the study.

**8.** As you ask the questions, keep in mind that they are designed to be used just as they are written. You may simply read them aloud. Or you may prefer to express them in your own words. There may be times when it is appropriate to deviate from the study guide. For example, a question may have already been answered. If so, move on to the next question. Or someone may raise an important question not covered in the guide. Take time to discuss it, but try to keep the group from going off on tangents.

**9.** Avoid answering your own questions. If necessary, repeat or rephrase them until they are clearly understood. Or point out something you read in the leader's notes to clarify the context or meaning. An eager group quickly becomes passive and silent if they think the leader will do most of the talking.

**10.** Don't be afraid of silence. People may need time to think about the question before formulating their answers.

**11.** Don't be content with just one answer. Ask, "What do the rest of you think?" or "Anything else?" until several people have given answers to the question.

**12.** Acknowledge all contributions. Try to be affirming whenever possible. Never reject an answer. If it is clearly off-base, ask, "Which verse led you to that conclusion?" or again, "What do the rest of you think?"

**13.** Don't expect every answer to be addressed to you, even though this will probably happen at first. As group members become more at ease, they will begin to truly interact with each other. This is one sign of healthy discussion.

**14.** Don't be afraid of controversy. It can be very stimulating. If you don't resolve an issue completely, don't be frustrated. Move on and keep it in mind for later. A subsequent study may solve the problem.

**15.** Periodically summarize what the group has said about the passage. This helps to draw together the various ideas mentioned and gives continuity to the study. But don't preach.

**16.** At the end of the Bible discussion you may want to allow group members a time of quiet to work on an idea under "Now or Later." Then discuss what you experienced. Or you may want to encourage group members to work on these ideas between meetings. Give an opportunity during the session for people to talk about what they are learning.

**17.** Conclude your time together with conversational prayer, adapting the prayer suggestion at the end of the study to your group. Ask for God's help in following through on the commitments you've made.

**18.** End on time.

Many more suggestions and helps are found in *How to Lead a LifeGuide Bible Study.*

### Components of Small Groups

A healthy small group should do more than study the Bible. There are four components to consider as you structure your time together.

*Nurture.* Small groups help us to grow in our knowledge and love of God. Bible study is the key to making this happen and is the foundation of your small group.

*Community.* Small groups are a great place to develop deep friendships with other Christians. Allow time for informal interaction before and after each study. Plan activities and games that will help you get to know each other. Spend time having fun together going on a picnic or cooking dinner together.

*Worship and prayer.* Your study will be enhanced by spending time praising God together in prayer or song. Pray for each other's needs and keep track of how God is answering prayer in your group. Ask God to help you to apply what you are learning in your study.

*Outreach.* Reaching out to others can be a practical way of applying what you are learning, and it will keep your group from becoming self-focused. Host a series of evangelistic discussions for your friends or neighbors. Clean up the yard of an elderly friend. Serve at a soup kitchen together, or spend a day working on a Habitat house.

Many more suggestions and helps in each of these areas are found in *Small Group Idea Book.* Information on building a small group can be found in *Small Group Leaders' Handbook* and *The Big Book on Small Groups* (both from InterVarsity Press). Reading through one of these books would be worth your time.

### Study 1. The Secure Mother. Ephesians 1:3-14.

*Purpose:* To help mothers constantly live in their secure identity in the person and work of Jesus Christ.

**Question 2.** Paul uses active verbs in describing God's love toward his people. He also uses the passive voice to describe the blessings we receive from God the Father. Help the group look thoroughly in the text to find all the blessings of God: he chose us, he predestined us, he's given us grace, and he's made known to us the mystery of his will. Because of him, we're included in Christ, we have redemption, we have the forgiveness of sins, and we're marked with the seal of the Holy Spirit. Guide the group to simply list the blessings at this point and not enter into a discussion about what they mean or how each blessing is seen in our lives. This will help the group see the overwhelming goodness of God in all that he has done for his people through Christ.

**Question 3.** Noticing the language that Paul uses to describe God here is important in helping the group embrace the truths of who they are in Christ. Paul uses words and phrases such as "in love," "pleasure," "riches," "lavished," "good pleasure," "freely," "wisdom and understanding," and "glorious." All these expressions reveal a God who cherishes his people and desires to lavish his love and grace on each person. It is crucial for mothers to understand how abundant God's love for them is.

**Question 4.** The image of adoption is perhaps the most powerful image in this passage. If there are women present who have been adopted or who have adopted children themselves, you might invite them to share. Hearing about their journeys might enhance the group's understanding of God's heart of love. Adoption is a final, legal act; an adopted child can be certain of not only their rights as a child but also the relationship with the parent. God's adoption of us means we can let go of trying to please him through our spiritual disciplines, accomplishments or success as a parent and instead rest in God, confident of our place as his child.

**Question 5.** This question is a more practical follow-up to question four, and it gets at the heart of our insecurity as women and mothers. If people are having difficulty answering, you might ask, "How do you feel or respond when your child misbehaves around others or when they fail at something?" This question may feel out of place, but it is designed to lead into question 6.

**Question 7.** Feel free to linger on this question, as it may be an emotional and even painful one for people to answer. Encourage the group to listen as well as stop and pray, if needed. You could also suggest meeting at another time to pray for women who are really wrestling with this question.

**Question 8.** God's will is to bring all things in heaven and earth into unity— and to work out everything in conformity to that plan. God is about the redemption of the world and his people through his Son, Jesus.

**Question 9.** The fact that God's purpose is to bring redemption and unity to all things and to bring all things under Christ means that he is actively working in our children's lives to mold them and bring them into relationship with Christ. So the pain, suffering and mistakes that we and our children make can be redeemed as God works to bring unity to all things. Having this broader perspective can keep us from being overwhelmed by the smaller details of our lives.

**Question 10.** If we can cultivate our ability to listen to the Holy Spirit, then, for example, in the times when we're tempted to respond to our children in anger or with manipulation, we might hear his tender exhortation and respond differently. There is great comfort in knowing that we're not alone in trying to control our anger with our children or in trying to respond to them with wisdom and love. The Spirit is also empowering us when we have to make tough decisions about discipline or when we have to respond to the pain of our children's choices. You may want to brainstorm together ways that each person can open themselves up more to the voice of the Holy Spirit. One suggestion is spending more time in prayer not only for our children but also for the ability to hear the Spirit and the courage to obey him. Practicing stopping in the midst of conflict or discussion with your kids and asking the Holy Spirit for direction is also a good practice that can remind us we're not alone.

### Study 2. The Healing Mother. Mark 5:21-43

*Purpose:* To help mums recognize how their own woundedness and pain affect their ability to parent in healthy ways, and to acknowledge the places that need healing and redemption through Christ.

**Personal Reflection and Group Discussion.** A crucial part of motherhood is being able to look inside ourselves and identify the places where we are operating out of emotional deficits or responding out of brokenness, and to continually open our lives to the healing power of Jesus so that he can redeem and bring health to us as people. When this happens, there is a break in the cycle of pain and hurt in our families.

**Question 1.** Make sure the group identifies Jairus, the woman and Jesus as the main characters.

**Question 2.** Jairus is a synagogue leader, which was a prominent position in the Jewish community. That fact, along with the possible presence of servants in his household (v. 35), means he was probably wealthy. We also know that he is a father who loves his daughter. The woman is most likely Jewish and probably poor from paying doctors. And, due to the Levitical law regarding bleeding (see Lev 15:19-30), she's been an outcast for the twelve years of her disease; anyone who touched her would be considered unclean and would have to follow certain practices in order to be restored to a state of purity. Essentially she is a woman in emotional and physical pain, without connection or reputation.

**Question 3.** Mark tells this story in a masterful way by juxtaposing these two people. In every category Jairus and the woman seem to be complete opposites: male/female, rich/poor, prominent/outcast, supported/alone, father/childless. Yet they share some similarities in their grief, suffering and desperation. Having exhausted their own strength and all other avenues of help, they are both feeling desperate and thus turn to the only person left who they think can help: Jesus.

It is also important to spend some time looking at the different ways Jairus and the woman come to Jesus. Jairus comes in a very public way, falling at the feet of Jesus, which would have been an undignified thing for a community leader to do. In contrast, the woman comes in private, fearful of being seen or noticed since she is breaking the Levitical law by coming into a public arena with crowds. Think about the mortification and fear she would have felt when Jesus stops and tries to identify her.

**Question 5.** You may have to give some examples or share first to start the discussion, so it'd be good for you as the leader to have thought about this question ahead of time. The group will respond to the level of vulnerability that you're willing to engage.

**Question 6.** This is a very important question because it connects our own wounds and deficits to the ways we parent and interact with our children. Give the group a few minutes of quiet to reflect, and encourage them to answer this question honestly.

**Question 7.** Some women in your group may need to lay specific past experiences before Jesus and pray for healing on their own. Others may need specific prayer times with this group or a prayer group. Still others may need to seek additional help from a pastor or counselor. Try to help the group members think about specific steps that might be needed to address, identify and acknowledge the pain that is there.

**Question 8.** Sometimes we need a picture of hope in order to face the difficult road ahead. Contemplating how our motherhood could change if our own deficits are redeemed and healed can provide us with that. Try to paint a picture of health and freedom for the group. Specific pictures might be not having to control every decision for a child or the peace that comes in letting a child be who they are instead of who we want them to be, or the lack of rebellious behavior in a child because they do not feel manipulated, or the health that comes from a wise context of discipline.

**Question 9.** Interestingly, Jairus came in public but Jesus brought healing in private, whereas the woman came in private but Jesus healed her in a very public way. You might ask the group why they think this is the case. I believe Jesus needed to restore the woman in public because she had not only physical wounds but also emotional and social wounds. Her public healing restored her socially to the community. Jairus, apparently, needed a private experience of healing in order for Jesus to heal his wounds. There is less evidence in the text as to why Jesus kept this healing private. The important aspects of this question are that Jesus knew exactly what each person needed and that he met that person in their desperation, bringing healing to the whole person.

**Question 10.** Jesus restored the woman and Jairus's daughter physically in the healing of their bodies, but he also cared passionately about the emotional wounds of the woman and Jairus. If Jesus hadn't publicly restored the woman, her humiliation would have stayed with her in many ways, even if her physical body was healed. Jesus also affirmed her faith in his power and authority; in so doing he was affirming the condition of her soul.

Jairus also experiences Jesus' love and grace on multiple levels. Jesus had already encountered skepticism, accusation and doubt from the teachers of the law. It's very possible that Jairus, as a synagogue leader, had felt that opposition to Jesus. Yet he risked his reputation in seeking out Jesus. There is affirmation for him spiritually too, as well as emotional healing at being given back his daughter. Jesus responds to both Jairus and the woman without condemnation or shock. He looks beyond the physical to the heart and receives both of them exactly where they are. His love and grace toward them is evident in the story.

**Question 11.** Many times we become accustomed to our pain, and it is far more frightening to let go of it and face the unknown than to continue living with it. This may be a very hard question for the group to engage. It will be important for you as the leader to be patient and to help those in the group identify what it is exactly that they are afraid of.

**Question 12.** The goal here is to give the group some way of responding to all they have uncovered. Without specific steps in place to continue the reflection or go deeper, it will be too easy for people to fall back on old patterns and become discouraged. This question also gives the group ways of checking in with each other and coming alongside one another in this process of healing.

### Study 3. The Trusting Mother. Matthew 6:25-34.

*Purpose:* To aid women in identifying the anxieties that have power in their lives and to highlight the alternative: a focus on the kingdom of God.

**Personal Reflection and Group Discussion.** These questions are important for the rest of the study, as they raise awareness of the triggers and effects of worry in our lives. Anxiety and worry can cause physical damage to our bodies, create conditioned emotional responses and spread anxiety to our children, burdening them with the same patterns of worry.

**Question 1.** Jesus describes worry about our life, which he further articulates as worry about what to eat and drink. He also mentions worry about the body and further describes that as manifesting itself in worry over what to wear. In addition, Jesus separates out worry about the future by highlighting worry about tomorrow. Challenge the group to look through the whole passage and to dig deeper than merely answering with "life" and "the body."

**Question 2.** Again, guide the group to look through the whole passage to answer. Jesus uses the birds of the air and flowers as a comparison/contrast to humanity. The contrasts are what's key to this question, however. It does not seem that birds or flowers focus on survival, dwell on it or experience anxiety related to it, nor do they chase after the things that will bring them worth or identity. Instead, they live freely, focusing on being what they were created to be.

**Question 3.** In Jesus' day, many people lived subsistence lives; in their agrarian society the accessibility of food and drink was more unstable. People were constantly worried about their daily physical needs, especially because they had less of an ability to store away, preserve or ration food. Thus, Jesus' challenge to not worry about food and drink was essentially an instruction to trust him with their physical survival. In our present world there are, of course, millions of people still struggling to survive and needing daily provision of food and drink. But this question will most likely mean something different for your group—maybe anxiety about our health or the health and safety of our families or worry related to getting older and the loss of physical abilities we used to have.

**Question 4.** This question might seem too straightforward, but the goal is to have the group wrestle with several things. One is getting at the source of our worry and what we believe worrying will do. For so many people, including mothers, worrying gives the appearance of somehow taking control; it's often our attempt to avoid pain and make life function according to our perceptions and desires, as Jesus points out. In addition, sometimes we worry because we view it as a sign of love; if we don't worry, do we really care? Jesus' words challenge this perception as well. Laying down our worry is a sign of trust and faith in our heavenly Father. It's also a sign that we intellectually, emotionally and spiritually understand that we can do nothing to control the events of life. Our hope and trust must be in the Father and not in the specifics of life unfolding just as we planned.

**Question 5.** This is similar to question three, but because Jesus seems to distinguish between worries about life and worries about the body, it's worth looking at separately. Clothing is certainly an issue of shelter and of humility in covering nakedness, but Jesus may be getting at something deeper in terms of identity and worth. What are the areas that cause us anxiety and worry related to "clothing ourselves" (i.e., our worth)? One of the deepest worries for women can be body image. Our "clothes" can be our physical bodies and the struggle to find worth in Jesus' love for us, not in how we measure up to the next woman. When Jesus calls us to lay aside worry about our clothes, then, he could be asking us to lay aside the perpetual drive to change how we look, how much we weigh and how we compare physically to one another. In verse 25 Jesus asks the question, "Isn't the body more important than the clothes?" We might apply that to our body image. Isn't it more important for our body to function as it was created to than for it to be a specific size or shape? Jesus is calling us to lay down our worry about these things and let the Father "clothe" us.

**Question 6.** Jesus' instructions not to worry come just after his warning about the impossibility of simultaneously striving after money and the kingdom of God. Since financial worries are one of the biggest sources of difficulty for spouses and families, it seems safe to say that Jesus' words in verses 25-34 include anxiety related to money as well. Guide the group into specific discussions about financial anxiety if the topic has not already come up in previous questions.

**Questions 7-9.** There ought to be a distinct difference between the way the people of God live and the way those who don't believe in him live, and one of the biggest differences, according to Jesus in this passage, is what we strive after ("run after," v. 32)—in other words, what we are focused on and what we make decisions based on.

These questions are important for mothers. Too often, we can become so focused on "running after"—providing every opportunity for success and accomplishment for our children and addressing our own identity deficits through our children—that the work of the kingdom is left out of our lives. What does it look like to choose compassion over competition on the sidelines of our children's sporting events? What does it look like to choose mercy over comfort in getting to know the families of other children at school? What does it mean to choose justice for someone else instead of success?

### Study 4. The Wonder-Filled Mother. Psalm 139:1-18.

*Purpose:* To help women recapture a sense of wonder at their children and at themselves because they embrace the Lord's knowing presence with them and their children.

**Question 1.** The psalmist begins by recounting the depth of God's knowledge of us—the intimate and experiential understanding that he has of each of us—using descriptive verbs like *know, search, perceive, discern, hem in.*

The psalmist then moves from God's knowledge to God's presence and the constancy of it. In verses 11-12, the author expands the idea of presence by describing God's presence as light that dispels any darkness. Verses 13-18 then move to a discussion of God's careful, detailed and intimate creation.

**Question 3.** There is a change in the voice from the first section to the second. The first section uses the second-person singular voice and focuses entirely on the activity of God. *You* is repeated eight times, and the verbs are intimate and describe the understanding and knowledge of God. In verses 7-12, the personal pronouns *I* and *me* are frequently repeated. This creates an emphasis on God's constant presence with the psalmist. God is present with the psalmist no matter his circumstances or location. Between the depth of God's knowledge in verses 1-5 and the continual presence of the Lord in verses 7-12, the psalmist is overwhelmed by the nature of God, who is omniscient (all-knowing) and omnipresent (present in all places). The last thing that is revealed about God in these verses is his character in contrast to the darkness. Darkness, often used as a symbol of pain, fear or death, is nothing compared to the power of God. His power, presence and goodness completely overwhelms the darkness.

**Question 4.** Encourage the group to be honest about their emotional reactions to the verses. Some people are comforted by the truth of God's presence with them at all times and in all places, but others might be filled with a sense of anxiety. Knowing that we can't escape God's presence can stir up feelings of panic depending on a person's overall perspective of God the Father. For example, if someone feels that God is "watching" and waiting for mistakes or failure, then the thought of God's constant presence can be frightening or disheartening. You might need to spend a few moments on this question so that any women who express panic or anxiety over God's constant presence can start to think about and process where that emotion comes from.

**Question 7.** These verses teach us a specific worldview—that God is not distant and unconcerned, but is intimately involved and active in creation. These verses remind us that God's creative acts in the world are good and are not accidental. But this worldview can be difficult at times, which can be another area of pain for women. We intellectually embrace that we are wonderfully made, but internally we tend to focus on the areas of our bodies and lives that we don't like or are ashamed of. We can be very hard on ourselves and, consequently, have a hard time believing that God has created us wonderfully or beautifully. The unfortunate result of this can be that our dislike of ourselves bleeds into our parenting, as we often end up focusing on the very same aspects in our children that we don't like in ourselves. Our children feel this. As we come to accept ourselves and how God has created us—body shape and all—we will be able to pass on to our children, especially our daughters, a sense of confidence as well.

**Study 5. The Growing Mother. Romans 12:1-8.**

*Purpose:* To encourage women to take practical steps in using their spiritual gifts in the work of God's kingdom and to choose spiritual disciplines that will keep them connected to God and growing in faith.

**Question 1.** Help the group see the repetition of Paul's negative exhortation "do not." He uses this negative two times, and each time it is significant to the development of his idea The contrast between the pattern of the world and being transformed is important, as is the contrast between "many" and "one." The idea of unity in the midst of diversity as Paul describes it here related to spiritual gifts is crucial to understanding the text as well. Spend time on this question, because it will help the group see how the passage fits together. Paul's thoughts develop from being a sacrifice to being transformed and then to being realistic about our individual role and using the gifts God has given in the context of the body.

**Question 2.** Paul uses "body" to mean our entire self, and the image is that of laying an animal on the altar of the temple to be completely given over to the Lord. For animals in the Old Testament sacrificial system this meant literal death, of course, but for us, giving our whole selves over to God actually brings abundant life. The key is being willing to offer everything! This means our sins, yes, but also our physical bodies, our ambitions, our dreams, our hopes as well as our fears, our insecurities, and even future plans and intentions. All this is offered to the Lord so that he can take it, transform it, and use it for his purpose in the world and to bring us into a deeper experience of the abundant life that Jesus promises.

**Question 3.** This may be a difficult question for group members to answer, but try to persist in the discussion. The intent of the question is to help people identify possible places in their own lives where they have pulled back even though they sense that God may be calling them to something. For example, perhaps someone has set aside her own ministry gifts since becoming a mother. There are so many ways in which women are tempted to hold on to things instead of placing them on the altar and letting God decide what he wants to do. Encourage the group to think about their time, energy, gifts, talents, relationships, physical possessions, physical selves, fears, ministries and passions. In response to God's life-saving mercy, we are called to offer all of these aspects of life to the Lord, to be a sacrifice that is not consumed in death but one that is brought into more abundant life.

**Question 5.** We don't grow by working harder or by trying to please God by performance. Instead, our minds are renewed by opening ourselves up to the power of the Holy Spirit and allowing his transformative work to reign. Many times the context for this to happen is spiritual disciplines such as Scripture study, prayer, worship, fellowship, fasting, giving, solitude or meditation. Serving and ministering are also key spiritual disciplines. For balanced and full spiritual growth, we need both the internal and external disciplines. It is critical to remember, though, that it is not the discipline itself that has the power to renew our minds. Rather, they give the Holy Spirit access and space in our lives to work.

**Question 6.** It is incredibly easy for us as busy, overwhelmed and fatigued mothers to neglect the very disciplines that would energize, encourage and ground us. Naming the consequences that come from doing so can help us make the disciplines a priority. The ironic piece of this progression is that when we as mothers neglect our own spiritual growth because we don't have time or because we don't want to say no to our children, we end up hurting our children more because our hearts and minds are not being renewed and transformed and we're not growing in wisdom, compassion or love.

**Question 8.** Paul's words here are not just about personal spiritual growth; they are also about the unity of the body of Christ. The church was made up of both Jews and Gentiles, and the tendency was to separate along those lines. In addition, it was easy for believers to value themselves more highly than others based on what kinds of spiritual gifts the Spirit had apportioned out. Paul exhorts them not to do so. Each believer is different, he reminds us, but none is valued more than another Indeed, difference and diversity are crucial to the body, but it is only when the believers are being renewed and are not conforming to the patterns of the world that this diversity can be embraced and celebrated for the good of the body.

**Question 9.** Women tend to struggle with one of two extremes: feeling insecure or feeling superior. Women also tend to struggle with comparing ourselves to each other incessantly. We compare our looks, our children's accomplishments, our physical possessions, our own accomplishments, our choices in life, our income levels, our degrees and every other aspect of our lives. We also wrestle with the unrealistic expectation that we can and should be able to handle all things and be "supermums."

**Question 10.** Verse 5 is crucial in understanding the unity in the midst of diversity that Paul is highlighting. If we use our gifts in individualistic ways, we are tempted to arrogance about our own talents, ignoring what others bring to the community. Yet, if we recognize that in being one body in Christ we set aside some of our individualism, we will come to understand that we belong to one another. We are one body, one family, and only when we all contribute do we function as one. There is something very powerful about living in the truth that we are connected to one another in Christ.

**Study 6. The Free Mother. Psalm 131.**

*Purpose:* To encourage mothers to release their unhealthy expectations about specific ways God must bless them or their children and embrace a childlike trust in God's sovereignty.

**Question 1.** The whole psalm is constructed around a major literary contrast that is hinted at by looking at the specific words. Words such as *proud* and *haughty* are set against words such as *calmed, quieted* and *content.*

**Question 2.** The psalmist is describing through negation a prideful, arrogant, ambitious person who is concerned about many things, even things that are far beyond that person's ability. The first verse gives the reader a sense of someone caught up in pride and arrogance who is taking charge and taking control of life.

**Question 3.** This is an important distinction to make, because the psalm is definitely casting a negative light on the idea of ambition in verse 1, but elsewhere in Scripture, Paul (for example) seems to encourage us to be ambitious and strive for what's ahead (see Phil 3:14). At root, the ambition the psalmist is criticizing is humanity kicking God out of the picture and attempting to rule without him. It occurs when people become proud and arrogant and think that they can control their lives and destinies. Aspiration, on the other hand, is recognizing that we are created but not the Creator. Yes, we are made in the image of God, but we are to respond to God's commands in obedience and relationship. Aspiration means humbly understanding both that we are loved and cared for by an eternal God and that we are created to grow in that which God has called us to without trying to control, manipulate or rule.

**Question 4.** Weaned children are those who have gradually begun to see their mother as more than the means of satisfying desire, and have started to love their mother for her own sake; they're happy to simply be in their mother's presence. It might be helpful to discuss the process of weaning as well. It's stormy and difficult as children are denied what they want and as the instant satisfaction of needs and desires is withheld. The process is so important, though, because what seemed essential to the children becomes no longer essential. While we still satisfy our children's needs at that point, of course, their joy is in the relationship with us, not merely in what we can give to them.

**Question 5.** It might be necessary to refer the group back to the discussion of extremes in question two. We can often be filled with arrogance and pride and try to take control of our own lives, but we can also slip into thinking that we are merely infantile children who just want God to comfort us and fulfill all our needs and wants. In other words, instead of developing a strong relationship with God—trusting in his character and love for us and enjoying his presence—we see God as a vending machine who is only in our lives to meet our every whim. We need to trust in who God is, not in what he provides or does not provide for us, and we desire God for himself, not as the means of fulfilling our every wish and desire. Help the group distinguish between these different kinds of trust.

**Questions 7-9.** As mothers, we have a tendency to want everything to be perfect: We want our kids to succeed academically and socially. We also have very high expectations of ourselves. We feel we should be able to work, organize, manage the family, spend quality time with our kids, be healthy, look great and accomplish amazing things. The contentment that the psalmist speaks about is a deep breath—a release of expectations about how God will bless us and our kids. It's a picture of us as mothers being free of the guilt and the anxiety, free of the striving and the need to control.

### Study 7. The Humble Mother. Luke 18:9-14.

*Purpose:* To urge women to live in grace toward one another, letting go of the arrogance and judgment that helps them feel more secure about themselves.

**Question 1.** Jesus' audience included people (most likely Pharisees themselves) who had two characteristics. First, they were confident that they'd be found righteous by God. We can extrapolate from this that they had been following the law and adhering to the commands of the covenant; they were "good" people. But they were trusting that their own good behavior was what kept them in relationship with God. The second characteristic is that they "looked down on everybody else," as Luke puts it. We get the sense from the text that the two characteristics are closely connected. Self-righteousness comes from believing that I have accomplished something without any help or assistance from someone else. It's easy to then expect that everyone else can do the same; self-righteousness leads to arrogance, and arrogance leads to judgment and critique of others. What can be overlooked is the next step in the pattern. Judgment and critique of others leads to strained and broken relationships and often isolation.

**Question 2.** It is not important to discuss all the small details about the Pharisees and the structure of Jewish life and authority, but it is helpful to understand a bit about who these people were. The Pharisees were the authorized teachers of Jesus' time. They exercised their influence through the Sanhedrin (the supreme Jewish religious, political and legal council in Jerusalem), the synagogues and the schools. They were very pious people and followed the law religiously. The tax collectors were Jewish people who worked for the oppressive ruling power—the Roman authorities. They were employed by the Romans to collect from their fellow countrymen the taxes that Israel owed to Rome. Because they worked for the power that ruled and oppressed the Jewish people, the tax collectors were viewed as traitors and treated as outcasts by the Jewish people. The tax collectors were also notorious for collecting more than was actually owed, thereby filling their own pockets with the money of their fellow Israelites. They were therefore also considered "sinners" by the Jewish people and by the Jewish authorities.

**Question 3.** It is clear from the very beginning of the Pharisee's prayer that he views himself as better and more worthy than others, and he points to his behavior as the standard by which he assesses his worthiness. The crucial piece to grasp is that the Pharisee's prayer is focused completely on *himself* and on what *he* has either done or not done. There is no mention of him receiving any aid or assistance in following the law; he clearly believes the achievement and success are solely his. So he has set himself apart from everyone else. He sees the differences between himself and others, not the similarities.

**Question 4.** The differences between the two men are profound. Where the Pharisee is arrogant and self-righteous, the tax collector is truthful and repentant. He feels the weight of his sin and is bowed down by it; beating his chest is a gesture of anguish, repentance and pain. The Pharisee is focused on his own accomplishments and behavior whereas the tax collector pleads for mercy and the grace of God. The Pharisee is isolated from others because of his judgment of them, whereas the tax collector feels unworthy to be in the presence of God. He cannot even raise his head up to heaven, and he doesn't feel worthy enough to approach the place where others pray but "stands at a distance." His physical demeanor is also the opposite of the Pharisee's. He does not look up, which gives the impression that he feels unworthy, embarrassed, perhaps, or guilty.

**Question 5.** This question moves the group from an academic engagement with the passage to a personal reflection on the tendency to be self-righteous in our parenting or to be overwhelmed with unworthiness. Encourage the group to honestly evaluate the temptation to be self-righteous. Mothers are competitive, and we tend to compare ourselves endlessly with other mothers. Comparison and competition focus on and rely on our own accomplishments and behaviors and those of our children. There are further questions in this study on these issues, so do not feel the need to push the group. This question should open the door for personal application and, hopefully, honest discussion.

**Question 6.** If the group is having trouble answering, direct them to answer the personal reflection question at the beginning of the study. Sometimes the things that we brag about or are proud of in terms of our children are the things that we feel self-righteous about. For example, I may take pride in my daughter's good grades and positive behavior, thinking that it's all a result of my exceptional abilities as a parent, when in reality, it's because of God's mercy. I had a positive childhood and functional parents. I had the financial resources to offer her extracurricular opportunities. I had the ability to be flexible in my work schedule so I could attend her school functions and be at home after school. All of those aspects of my parenting are more a result of God's grace and goodness to me than my own accomplishment. Yet when I see someone else's child misbehaving or making poor choices, my first reaction is to judge them and say to myself, *God, thank you that I am not like that mother.*

Discussion for this question may become complicated, because you'll be wrestling with whether it's acceptable to be proud and with what we can take responsibility for and what we can't. The goal is to help the group realize that we often "look down" on other mothers due to their choices or to their children's behaviors or accomplishments. We need to see that when we do this, we are the Pharisee trusting in his own righteousness and living in arrogance. We are called to be the tax collector, constantly recognizing our need for the grace and mercy of Christ and aware of our sin and brokenness.

**Question 7.** The answer that Jesus gives flips the understanding of being justified by God upside down. The law was the way to be declared righteous before God in the eyes of the Pharisees, who had, by the time of Jesus, become so caught up in the legalism of the law that they had expanded it into hundreds of smaller laws that governed every aspect of a person's life. The only way to be justified before God in their teaching was by obeying every single aspect of the covenant and the expanded laws. But here Jesus is explaining that humbling ourselves before God in an attitude of repentance is what's important. It's not about trying harder to do the right things but rather about throwing ourselves on the mercy of God. That's why the tax collector was the one who was declared righteous.

There may be women in your group who have not really grasped the gospel message this way. Some might still see the Christian life as a life of following rules and trying harder to behave correctly. The good news is that even though we are sinful and broken and we cannot follow Jesus in our own power, the Holy Spirit lives in us and empowers us to follow Jesus.

**Question 9.** This question gets at the consequences of living like the Pharisee and the tax collector. Encourage women to talk about relationships they have had that have been positive or negative because of their comparison with, competition with or judgment of others. Also encourage them to talk about how wonderful a relationship has been when they have been able to be truthful, honest and humble.

**Question 10.** The freedom comes in being released from the pressure to compare ourselves to other women and the pressure to compete.

### Study 8. The Connected Mother. Colossians 3:1-17.

*Purpose:* To help mums commit to participation in community so that they can extend and receive compassion, kindness, humility and patience, as well as share their burdens and the anxieties of parenting with others.

**Question 1.** The structure of this passage is based on the cause-and-effect relationships that Paul explains, so it will be important for the group to identify these. Encourage the group to keep looking until they have truly seen most of the following connections: since you have been raised—set your hearts on things above (v. 1); set your minds on things above—for you died, and your life is now hidden with Christ in God (vv. 2-3); put to death—because you have been raised with Christ (the relationship is based on the truth of vv. 1-4); because of these (the earthly nature)—the wrath of God is coming (v. 6); since you have taken off your old self and put on the new self—do not lie to each other (vv. 9-10); because of all these truths in verses 1-11—clothe yourselves (v. 12); since you were called to peace—let the peace of Christ rule in your hearts (v. 15).

**Question 2.** Paul uses stark contrasts to encourage the church to remember that the spiritual truth about who they are has changed dramatically and that they are no longer tied to their past. The church has a new reality, and it is in this new reality they are to live. The Colossians were grounded in earthly things in the past. They were not raised up, nor were their minds and hearts set on heavenly things. They were slaves to their earthly nature, which was characterized by evil desires and greed, by sexual immorality, impurity, lust and idolatry. They were destined for God's wrath and were ruled by anger, rage, malice, slander, filthy language and lies.

**Question 3.** The truth about their present reality is crucial for the Colossians to understand. It has changed in the spiritual realm, which means their behavior and practices can change. They are new people. In other words, the Colossians can now put on a new self, since they have been raised with Christ. Their salvation has been secured by Christ, and the old self no longer rules and reigns in them. The new self is being renewed in the knowledge of the Creator.

**Question 4.** The first section of this text revolves around the verb *set.* It is an action verb and focuses on the hierarchy of the earthly and heavenly realms. "Setting" implies carefully placing something somewhere or initiating an action or process. The Colossians are being encouraged to actively place their minds and hearts in a new condition, in a new place, beyond the earthly and sinful things around them. Because they died and were raised with Christ, they have the ability to place their hearts and minds on Christ. The second verb, *put,* is similar to the first verb. It is active and implies initiative on the part of the Colossians. The third verb is different from the first two because it's passive; *let* implies allowing action to happen to us. Paul specifically chooses a passive verb to point out that the peace and message of Christ already exist. The Colossians simply have to receive these things and allow them to rule in their lives.

**Question 6.** It is crucial to remember that this letter is written to a body of believers and not to individual believers. The list of earthly, sinful behaviors that Paul describes in verses 5 to 8—behaviors that used to characterize the Colossians—are ones that damage and destroy relationships and community. Verse 11, then, is the new framework by which they're to understand community. In Christ, the old barriers and distinctions that divide people from one another in the world, such as ethnicity, nationality and position, no longer exist. In Paul's companion text in Galatians 3:28 he adds gender. These differences are part of God's creation and are to be celebrated, not used to judge, limit, marginalize and hate. Paul is helping the Colossians see that the overriding characteristic that will define the community of Christ is unity: Christ is all and is in all. When believers understand their position as new creations in Christ, when they put aside the behaviors of the old self that destroy and damage one another, and when they see every individual through the lens of unity in Christ, then true Christian community can flourish.

**Question 9.** So often as mothers we do not experience this kind of community, though we need it perhaps more than we ever have as we struggle with insecurity, impatience, depression, judgment, fatigue and so many other things. We may choose not to engage in community because of tiredness and busyness, or we may not want to be vulnerable in a season of insecurity. Sometimes our insecurity leads to judgment of other women and so we can't connect relationally to them. Or, if we are feeling insecure about choices we've made regarding our children, we may struggle to interact with other women who have chosen different paths. We can feel judged or condemned, and we can struggle with justification and anger toward each other. In these ways we live in the old self, focusing on the self-made distinctions and differences between us. Being vulnerable and admitting we are not sure about our decisions is therefore crucial for putting on the new self, as is setting aside our attitudes of superiority toward other women.

**Question 10.** This is a continuation of the previous question, but the goal here is to move the discussion from an abstract place to specifics. Encourage the group to talk about the specific ways in which each woman needs community. Since you are studying this in a group already, this is a great question to use as a way of evaluating your group and its depth of community. You might want to ask people how they would rate this group according to the characteristics of this passage.

**Question 11.** Women can be inherently critical and judgmental. We can focus on the negative things about ourselves and our families without realizing the destructive nature of that negativity for our spouse and children. Cultivating a heart of thankfulness, worship and gratitude can be life-saving for us and for our families. When we learn to see and express the positive qualities in our children and in ourselves, we build up and empower our children. Colossians 3:15-17 provides one of the most important reminders we can hear as mothers.

### Study 9. The Influencing Mother. 1 Thessalonians 2:1-12.

*Purpose:* To challenge women to be intentional about the ways in which they are influencing or not influencing their children according to the kind of people they desire their children to become.

**Question 1.** Paul affirms the Thessalonian believers for who they are in Christ and for their witness in the whole area of Macedonia and Achaia. He points out three characteristics, in particular: their faith in Christ, their love for Christ and for one another, and their hope in Christ, which have been lived out in the church through their work, labor and endurance. Even in times of persecution, they have labored and persevered. Paul goes on in verses 7-8 to explain how they have become models of the faith; people around them know who they are and who they are following. So, not only are they models of faith in Christ; they also seem to be engaging in an active life of evangelism. As we study chapter 2 we'll see what experiences and processes helped form these characteristics in the church.

**Question 2.** The tiny phrase "dared to tell" is packed with insight and challenge for us. Before coming to Thessalonica, Paul and his companions had been beaten, flogged and imprisoned in Philippi, but they had also experienced the power of the Holy Spirit in their miraculous release from prison (see Acts 16–17). And they were only able to stay a short time in Thessalonica because they were threatened by a Jewish mob. They escaped from there at night and moved on to ministry in Berea and Athens. With this historical context, help the group wrestle with what it means to dare to tell the gospel. To dare to do something implies courage, risk and uncertainty but also passion. Paul, Silas and Timothy were passionate about others knowing Christ, so they faced risk with courage and perseverance.

**Question 3.** We rarely, if ever, face the kinds of risks that Paul, Silas and Timothy faced when they were sharing the gospel, but we do face challenges. Help the group engage this question on a personal level. Being embarrassed, losing friendships, being labeled or being disrespected might all be reasons given. Or maybe group members feel insecure about their spiritual knowledge or "evangelism skills" and are thus afraid they'll "fail." Help the group unpack the concept of taking risks and doing something "daring," and then push them to really specifically look at what it might mean for them to "dare to tell."

**Question 4.** Paul wants to be very sure that the Thessalonians know that the amount of time and energy they invested in the church came from a place of pure motives. In the ancient world (and in the modern world) people often acted out of impure motives in order to gain resources. They would manipulate, deceive and make money, or increase their authority (see Craig Keener, *IVP Bible Background Commentary: New Testament* [Downers Grove, IL: InterVarsity Press, 1993], pp. 586-88). In contrast, the ultimate motivation of Paul, Silas and Timothy was pleasing God, not others or themselves. This is a crucial truth that we all need to wrestle with in our lives. Are we acting out of a desire to please others, to increase our own reputations and positions, or to establish our authority? Or are we being obedient to care and minister for others in a way that pleases God only?

**Question 5.** This question is a tough one for women to think about in terms of their parenting. It may help to frame the discussion in terms of who we are trying to please. Often it's someone other than God. We want our children to like us and enjoy us, so we flatter them and neglect the discipline and structure they need. Or we might manipulate them to do what we want to serve our own agendas and desires. In those times, we harm our children and damage the relationship we have with them. It is not our call as parents to make sure our children feel good or like us. We are called by God to be their mother first, not their friend. When we forget who we should look to for praise and affirmation, that distinction gets turned upside down.

**Question 6.** Paul uses four main images of the family in these verses: young children, mothers, siblings and fathers. In verse 7 he ends his discussion of motives with the contrast of someone who is manipulating, flattering, and asserting rights and authority and a young child. Young children are not in a position to assert their authority but rather are to be humble with the adults in their lives. Paul is saying that instead of manipulating the believers to do what they wanted and instead of grasping at titles or authority as apostles in order to motivate the believers, they humbled themselves as young children and relied not on status but on relationship (see Keener, *IVP Bible Background Commentary*, pp. 586-88).

Paul further develops this model of discipleship by using the images of a nursing mother. (Note that in Paul's use of a nursing mother and a father in this passage, he is not trying to say that all mothers exhibit certain qualities nor all fathers; rather, he's using some general characteristics to illustrate the way the three men invested in the believers.) A nursing mother nurtures and loves her children. Paul is saying that the three of them did not just speak the message of Christ but also lived out the love of Christ in a nurturing, compassionate relationship.

Paul also uses the terms "brothers" (or "brothers and sisters," NIV 2011), which would have reminded the church that Paul, Silas and Timothy did not exert their position over them but came alongside them and toiled with them so as not to be a burden. This reference most likely refers to the three men not taking financial support from the church while they were ministering to them, but instead engaging in work in order to substantiate their pure motives (see Keener, *IVP Bible Background Commentary*, pp. 586-88).

The final familial image in these verses is that of a father. The characteristics of the father are slightly different but critical in mentoring and discipleship. Paul uses the words "encouraging," "comforting" and "urging" to describe this aspect of the relationship, implying that not only did the men love, care for and nurture the believers, but they also challenged and urged them forward in their spiritual growth, exhorting the believers to live worthy lives. The analogy of a father here would have reminded the believers that Paul and his companions cared that they were growing and deepening their faith in Christ.

**Question 8.** Verse 10 is a great illustration of the importance of modeling.

If Paul and his companions had taught what it meant to follow Jesus but their lives had reflected a different set of values, their impact on the believers would have been severely thwarted. It is the combination of modeling and articulation that is so powerful in the discipleship of others, our children included. Paul, Silas and Timothy could claim to be holy, blameless and righteous (which was quite the claim!). Through the power of the Holy Spirit, they were able to model what they hoped to see in the church at Thessalonica.

**Question 10.** This question is meant to be a heart question that helps the women in the group connect with their feelings about their relationship with their children. Some women may be filled with guilt because few of these elements are in place right now; they might need help processing those feelings of guilt. Others may long for this type of investment but are unsure how to move in this direction. Still others may be more positive and have examples of how they see this being lived out in their homes. Help the group refrain from judgment and avoid trying to "fix" one another so that people can share their heart and their gut response to the question. Encourage each woman in the place she's at.

**Question 11.** Because of the investment of Paul, Silas and Timothy, the Thessalonian church became known throughout their part of the world for their faith, love and hope as well as their witness. Encourage the group to think about the legacy that they hope to leave in the lives of their children.

### Study 10. The Joyful Mother. Philippians 4:4-9.

*Purpose:* To empower women to choose gratitude by focusing on what is noble, right, pure and lovely about their lives and their children instead of dwelling on negative aspects of family or circumstances.

**Question 1.** The difficulty in this passage is not intellectually understanding the content but applying it to our lives. This study will therefore seem more reflective in nature, with the questions leaning more on our response to the verses and on what it means to live in the reality of them. Help the group move from the intellectual to the personal in this study.

**Question 2.** It is amazing to think about how a person's life would change if he or she actually lived out these verses every day. The verses describe the foundational aspects of our faith: trust, peace and thankfulness through Christ. Being thankful in all circumstances keeps our focus off of ourselves and reduces our worry and anxiety, moving us toward being people of peace. Living in peace and thankfulness also contributes to physical health; many studies have shown the negative effects of stress and worry on our bodies. This pressure ultimately affects our spiritual lives as well.

**Question 3.** This is an important question because it gets at what rejoicing is and what it is not. "Rejoicing always" does not mean that we should put on a mask of happiness and ignore or deny the difficult things in life. Throughout this letter Paul refers to his own situation in prison. He doesn't deny it or shrink from implying that a life of persecution may be what is in store for the Philippian church. Instead, he calls them to have a bigger perspective than the present and to focus not on the current difficulty but on the joy of our salvation and the peace that Christ brings. Help the group understand this difference between a superficial happiness, where we ignore pain, and the deep rejoicing and thankfulness that come from having the correct perspective on life.

**Question 4.** Paul's perspective on prayer is that every situation can be brought before the Lord; no evaluative process is needed (by us or anyone else) to decide whether our concerns, desires or worries are "worthy" of being discussed with the Lord. Paul does, however, give us a framework for prayer here. We are to bring our requests to God through thanksgiving. That means that as we pray and intercede and petition God about our concerns and requests, we recognize how God has blessed us, how he is showing us his grace and how he is working in our lives.

**Question 5.** Paul says "the Lord is near," and there are two ways to view this small sentence: Paul might be referring to (1) the coming of the Lord or (2) the constant presence of Jesus. The kingdom that Jesus ushered in is both hear and not yet here. Since Jesus is near to us through the Spirit, it is instructive to discuss how this affects our daily lives. If we truly believe that the Lord is near to us at all times and in all places, then we will be more likely to look for his activity around us and in us—and we'll be more willing to open ourselves up to his voice. This, in turn, leads to a deeper sensitivity to the Spirit and an ability to see more of the things that bring us to joy and thanksgiving. This small phrase of Paul's is thus the critical piece in being able to set aside worry and anxiety.

**Question 9.** This might be a painful question for mothers because we so often focus on our children's faults and failures out of our desperate desire to see them succeed. Focusing on the negative does not just affect our children, though. It also has consequences in our own lives. When we obsess over negative aspects of our lives and our children's lives, we become slaves to worry and anxiety. Our thoughts and prayers become consumed, and we miss the amazing ways in which God is at work in us and in our children. We do not experience the kind of peace that "transcends all understanding" which Paul describes in this passage.

**Question 11.** Parenting is a crucible, so it's important to stop and reflect on what we have seen and learned about ourselves through the experience. This is an exercise in seeing the hand of God at work in redeeming and maturing us in Christ. Help the group honestly evaluate who they have become and how God has shaped them as a parent.

**Question 12.** It might be helpful to give the group some time to think, pray or journal before you discuss it.

*Patty Pell (M.A., Old Testament Studies, Denver Seminary) is pastor of community impact at Christ Community Church in Greeley, Colorado, where she lives with her husband, Scott, and their three children. She is the author of* Esther *and* Hospitality *in the LifeGuide® Bible Study series and a coauthor of* Small Group Leaders' Handbook.

# What should we study next?

*We have LifeGuides for . . .*

**Knowing Jesus**
*Advent of the Savior*
*Following Jesus*
*I Am*
*Abiding in Christ*
*Jesus' Final Week*

**Knowing God**
*Meeting God*
*God's Comfort*
*God's Love*
*The 23rd Psalm*
*Miracles*
*Distorted Images of God*

**Growing in the Spirit**
*Meeting the Spirit*
*Fruit of the Spirit*
*Spiritual Gifts*
*Spiritual Warfare*

**Looking at the Trinity**
*Images of Christ*
*Images of God*
*Images of the Spirit*

**Developing Disciplines**
*Christian Disciplines*
*God's Word*
*Hospitality*
*The Lord's Prayer*
*Prayer*
*Praying the Psalms*
*Sabbath*
*Worship*

**Deepening Your Doctrine**
*Angels*
*Christian Beliefs*
*The Cross*
*End Times*
*Good & Evil*
*Heaven*
*The Kingdom of God*
*The Story of Scripture*

**Seekers**
*Encountering Jesus*
*Jesus the Reason*
*Meeting Jesus*

**Leaders**
*Christian Leadership*
*Integrity*
*Elijah*
*Joseph*

**Shaping Your Character**
*Christian Character*
*Decisions*
*Self-Esteem*
*Parables*
*Pleasing God*
*Woman of God*
*Women of the New Testament*
*Women of the Old Testament*

**Living Fully at Every Stage**
*Singleness*
*Marriage*
*Parenting*
*Couples of the Old Testament*
*Couples of the New Testament*
*Growing Older & Wiser*

**Reaching Our World**
*Missions*
*Evangelism*
*Four Great Loves*
*Loving Justice*

**Living Your Faith**
*Christian Virtues*
*Forgiveness*

**Growing in Relationships**
*Christian Community*
*Friendship*